Books by W. S. Merwin

The Carrier of Ladders

.

. . . The bearer of the dead
Says to the carrier of ladders,
It is the day for carrying loads,
It is the day of trouble.

DAHOMEY SONG

The Carrier of Ladders

POEMS BY W. S. Merwin

New York *ATHENEUM* *1980*

Poems in this collection have appeared in *Abraxas; The Atlantic Monthly; Chelsea; Chicago Tribune; Harper's Bazaar; Harper's Magazine; The Hudson Review; The Iowa Review; The Journal of Creative Behavior; Kayak; Lillabulero; The Nation; New Directions Annual; The New Republic; The New York Quarterly; The New Yorker* (PLANE, THE DIFFERENT STARS, THE MOUNTAINS, THE HANDS, THE JUDGMENT OF PARIS, EDOUARD, ENVOY FROM D'AUBIGNÉ, THE WELL, THE BLACK PLATEAU, FEBRUARY, THE PORT, THE FREE, THE PRINTS, THE OLD ROOM, SNOWFALL, BANISHMENT IN WINTER, THE HULK, FEAR, SHORE, SECOND PSALM: THE SIGNALS, NOW IT IS CLEAR, FOURTH PSALM: THE CEREMENTS, THE WEB, LETTER); *Poetry* (DO NOT DIE, NOT THESE HILLS, ENCOUNTER, INSCRIPTION FACING WESTERN SEA, THE SADNESS, THE CALLING UNDER THE BREATH, SUNSET AFTER RAIN); *Quarterly Review of Literature; The Seventies; Sumac; Stonybrook; TriQuarterly.*

The epigraph facing the title page is a fragment from *For the Earth God*, a Dahomey song transcribed by Frances Herskovits, and originally published in Poetry, XLV (1934–1945).

The author wishes to thank the Rockefeller Foundation for a grant made to him in 1968, which was of great help during the time when some of these poems were being written.

for Dido

Contents

Contents

The Carrier of Ladders

PLANE

We hurtle forward and seem to rise

I imagine the deities come and go
without departures

and with my mind infinitely divided and hopeless
like a stockyard seen from above
and my will like a withered body muffled
in qualifications until it has no shape
I bleed in my place

where is no
vision of the essential nakedness of the gods
nor of that
nakedness the seamless garment of heaven

nor of any other
nakedness

Here
is the air

and your tears flowing on the wings of the plane
where once again I cannot
reach to stop them

and they fall away behind
going with me

TEACHERS

Pain is in this dark room like many speakers
of a costly set though mute
as here the needle and the turning

the night lengthens it is winter
a new year

what I live for I can seldom believe in
who I love I cannot go to
what I hope is always divided

but I say to myself you are not a child now
if the night is long remember your unimportance
sleep

then toward morning I dream of the first words
of books of voyages
sure tellings that did not start by justifying

yet at one time it seems
had taught me

THE OWL

These woods are one of my great lies
I pretend
oh I have always pretended they
were mine
I stumble among
the smaller lies
as this night falls and
of my pretenses likewise
some
and your voice
begins

who need no hope to
hunt here who
love me
I retreat before
your question as before my own
through old branches who
am I hiding
what creature in the bowels quaking
that should not be raised
against the night
crying its truth at last

No I who
love you
find while I can some light to crawl into
maybe
I will never answer
though your dark lasts as my own does
and your voice in it without hope
or need of it

The Owl

calling what I call calling
me me *You*
who are never there

THE DIFFERENT STARS

I could never have come to the present without you
remember that
from whatever stage we may again
watch it appear

with its lines clear
pain
having gone from there

so that we may well wonder
looking back on us here what tormented us
what great difficulty invisible
in a time that by then looks simple
and is irrevocable

pain having come from there
my love
I tend to think of division as the only evil
when perhaps it is merely my own

that unties
one day the veins one the arteries
that prizes less
as it receives than as it loses
that breaks the compasses
cannot be led or followed
cannot choose what to carry
into grief
even
unbinds will unbind
unbinds our hands
pages of the same story

what is it
they say can turn even this into wisdom
and what is wisdom if it is not
now
in the loss that has not left this place

oh if we knew
if we knew what we needed if we even knew
the stars would look to us to guide them

THE DEAD HIVE

The year still a child
but its sunlight
climbing for the first time in the poplars
pretending to be older
and the green has been lit in the east-sloping
pastures guarded
by nurses of shadow
a ghost has risen out of the earth
the unnamed warmth
saved for now

in the silence
one note is missing
I see
you nowhere I hear you nowhere
I climb to your hall you are nowhere
the flowers nod in the sun
like the blind
I knock
from the arcade of your portal
a fly steps out

I open the roof
I and the light
this is how it looks later
the city the dance the care
the darkness
the moment
one at a time
that is each one alone

as she
turns aside

obeying as always
and the accomplished limbs begin
welcoming
what does not move
and the eyes
go as far as they can
and wait

at the place where no one they know
can fail them

THE MOUNTAINS

There are days when I think the future sets
beyond the mountains
then I lay me down
in fear of departures

and a heavy
net drops on me when I wake
far
far in the night
borne on
and the whole air
around me crying for you
even
when you are still there

and a dog barking
beyond it
at an unknown distance

on and on

THE BRIDGES

Nothing but me is moving
on these bridges
as I always knew it would be
see moving on each of the bridges
only me

and everything that we have known
even the friends
lined up in the silent iron railings
back and forth
I pass like a stick on palings

the echo
rises from the marbled river
the light from the blank clocks crackles
like an empty film
where
are we living now
on which side which side
and will you be there

THE HANDS

. . . Ma non è cosa in terra
Che ti somigli . . .
LEOPARDI

I have seen them when there was
nothing else
small swollen flames lighting my way at
corners
where they have waited for
me

cut off from
everything they have made their way to me
one more day one more night leading
their blood and I wake
to find them lying at home
with my own

like a bird lying in its wings
a stunned
bird till they stir and
break
open cradling a heart not theirs
not mine
and I bend to hear who is beating

DO NOT DIE

In each world they may put us
farther apart
do not die
as this world is made I might
live forever

WORDS FROM A TOTEM ANIMAL

Distance
is where we were
but empty of us and ahead of
me lying out in the rushes thinking
even the nights cannot come back to their hill
any time

———

I would rather the wind came from outside
from mountains anywhere
from the stars from other
worlds even as
cold as it is this
ghost of mine passing
through me

———

I know your silence
and the repetition
like that of a word in the ear of death
teaching
itself
itself
that is the sound of my running
the plea
plea that it makes
which you will never hear
oh god of beginnings
immortal

———

I might have been right
not who I am
but alright
among the walls among the reasons
not even waiting
not seen
but now I am out in my feet
and they on their way
the old trees jump up again and again
strangers
there are no names for the rivers
for the days for the nights
I am who I am
oh lord cold as the thoughts of birds
and everyone can see me

———

Caught again and held again
again I am not a blessing
they bring me
names
that would fit anything
they bring them to me
they bring me hopes
all day I turn
making ropes
helping

———

My eyes are waiting for me
in the dusk
they are still closed
they have been waiting a long time
and I am feeling my way toward them

———

16

I am going up stream
taking to the water from time to time
my marks dry off the stones before morning
the dark surface
strokes the night
above its way
There are no stars
there is no grief
I will never arrive
I stumble when I remember how it was
with one foot
one foot still in a name

———

I can turn myself toward the other joys and their lights
but not find them
I can put my words into the mouths
of spirits
but they will not say them
I can run all night and win
and win

———

Dead leaves crushed grasses fallen limbs
the world is full of prayers
arrived at from
afterwards
a voice full of breaking
heard from afterwards
through all
the length of the night

———

I am never all of me
unto myself
and sometimes I go slowly
knowing that a sound one sound
is following me from world
to world
and that I die each time
before it reaches me

———

When I stop I am alone
at night sometimes it is almost good
as though I were almost there
sometimes then I see there is
in a bush beside me the same question
why are you
on this way
I said I will ask the stars
why are you falling and they answered
which of us

———

I dreamed I had no nails
no hair
I had lost one of the senses
not sure which
the soles peeled from my feet and
drifted away
clouds
It's all one
feet
stay mine
hold the world lightly

———

Stars even you
have been used
but not you
silence
blessing
calling me when I am lost

———

Maybe I will come
to where I am one
and find
I have been waiting there
as a new
year finds the song of the nuthatch

———

Send me out into another life
lord because this one is growing faint
I do not think it goes all the way

ANIMULA

Look soul
soul
barefoot presence
through whom blood falls as through
a water clock
and tears rise before they wake
I will take you

at last to
where the wind stops
by the river we
know
by that same water
and the nights are not separate
remember

QUINCE

The gentle quince blossoms open
they have no first youth
they look down on me
knowing me well
some place I had left

THE JUDGMENT OF PARIS

For Anthony Hecht

Long afterwards
the intelligent could deduce what had been offered
and not recognized
and they suggest that bitterness should be confined
to the fact that the gods chose for their arbiter
a mind and character so ordinary
albeit a prince

and brought up as a shepherd
a calling he must have liked
for he had returned to it

when they stood before him
the three
naked feminine deathless
and he realized that he was clothed
in nothing but mortality
the strap of his quiver of arrows crossing
between his nipples
making it seem stranger

and he knew he must choose
and on that day

the one with the gray eyes spoke first
and whatever she said he kept
thinking he remembered
but remembered it woven with confusion and fear
the two faces that he called father
the first sight of the palace
where the brothers were strangers

and the dogs watched him and refused to know him
she made everything clear she was dazzling she
offered it to him
to have for his own but what he saw
was the scorn above her eyes
and her words of which he understood few
all said to him *Take wisdom*
take power
you will forget anyway

the one with the dark eyes spoke
and everything she said
he imagined he had once wished for
but in confusion and cowardice
the crown
of his father the crowns the crowns bowing to him
his name everywhere like grass
only he and the sea
triumphant
she made everything sound possible she was
dazzling she offered it to him
to hold high but what he saw
was the cruelty around her mouth
and her words of which he understood more
all said to him *Take pride*
take glory
you will suffer anyway

the third one the color of whose eyes
later he could not remember
spoke last and slowly and
of desire and it was his
though up until then he had been
happy with his river nymph
here was his mind

filled utterly with one girl gathering
yellow flowers
and no one like her
the words
made everything seem present
almost present
present
they said to him *Take*
her
you will lose her anyway

it was only when he reached out to the voice
as though he could take the speaker
herself
that his hand filled with
something to give
but to give to only one of the three
an apple as it is told
discord itself in a single fruit its skin
already carved
To the fairest

then a mason working above the gates of Troy
in the sunlight thought he felt the stone
shiver

in the quiver on Paris's back the head
of the arrow for Achilles' heel
smiled in its sleep

and Helen stepped from the palace to gather
as she would do every day in that season
from the grove the yellow ray flowers tall
as herself

whose roots are said to dispel pain

24

EDOUARD

Edouard shall we leave
tomorrow
for Verdun again
shall we set out for the great days
and never be the same
never

time
is what is left
shall we start
this time in the spring
and they lead your cows out
next week to sell at the fair
and the brambles learn to scribble
over the first field

Edouard shall we have gone
when the leaves come out
but before the heat
slows the grand marches
days like those
the heights and the dying
at thy right hand
sound a long horn
and here the bright handles
will fog over
things will break and stay broken
in the keeping of women
the sheep get lost
the barns
burn unconsoled in the darkness

Edouard

Edouard what would you have given
not to go
sitting last night in by the fire
again
but shall we be the same
tomorrow night shall we not have gone
leaving the faces and nightingales
As you know we will live
and what never comes back will be
you and me

NOT THESE HILLS

Not these hills
are in my tongue
though I inquire of them again
which then
with their later season
on whose slopes my voice stirs
shining root
stream carrying small lights
to where one echo
waits

spring here
I am shown to me
as flies waking in the south walls
emerging from darkness one
at a time
dark
then gone
with nothing between them
but the sun

THE PIPER

It is twenty years
since I first looked for words
for me now
whose wisdom or something would stay me
I chose to
trouble myself about the onset
of this
it was remote it was grievous
it is true I was still a child

I was older then
than I hope ever to be again
that summer sweating in the attic
in the foreign country
high above the piper but hearing him
once
and never moving from my book
and the narrow
house full of pregnant women
floor above floor
waiting
in that city
where the sun was the one bell

It has taken me till now
to be able to say
even this
it has taken me this long
to know what I cannot say
where it begins
like the names of the hungry

Beginning
I am here
please
be ready to teach me
I am almost ready to learn

THE LAKE

Did you exist
ever

our clouds separated while it was still dark
then I could not sleep the sleep of a child
I got up to look for you
bringing my silence
all of it

no father in the house at least

I got my boat
that we had saved for each other
a white creature my
wise elder
You rustled as it slid
from shore

I lay there
looking down while the mist was torn
looking down
where
was the Indian village
said to be drowned there

one glimpse and I would have hung
fixed in its sky
when the dawn was gone
and the morning star
and the wind
and the sun
and the calling around you

30

THE CHURCH

High walls
pale brick like Babylon
above the cliff face
the house
of the lord

at the single window
up in the back
toward the river
the eyes I left
as a child there

everything gone now
the walls are down
the altar
only I am still standing
on the weedy rock in the wind
there is no building here

there are my hands
that have known between them
the bride
and call to her
wherever she is not wherever
she is *Hand*

hand

A CALM IN APRIL

Early mist
mountains like a rack of dishes
in a house I love
far mountains
last night the stars for a while
stopped trembling
and this morning the light will speak to me
of what concerns me

THE BIRDS ON THE
MORNING OF GOING

If I can say yes I
must say it to this
and now
trying to remember what the present
can bless with
which I know

from all other ages how little has come to me
that is breath
and nothing that is you

now I can see
I have been carrying this
fear
a blue thing
the length of my life asking *Is this*
its place
bringing it here

to the singing
of these brightening birds

they are neither dead nor unborn

a life opens it opens it is
breaking
does it find occasions for
every grief of its childhood
before it will have
done

oh my love here even the night turns back

ENVOY FROM D'AUBIGNÉ

Go book

go
now I will let you
I open the grave
live
I will die for us both

go but come again if you can
and feed me in prison

if they ask you why
you do not boast of me
tell them as they
have forgotten
truth habitually
gives birth in private

Go without ornament
without showy garment
if there is in you any
joy
may the good find it

for the others be
a glass broken in their mouths

Child
how will you
survive with nothing but your virtue
to draw around you
when they shout Die die

who have been frightened before
the many

I think of all I wrote in my time
dew
and I am standing in dry air

Here are what flowers there are
and what hope
from my years

and the fire I carried with me

Book
burn what will not abide your light

When I consider the old ambitions
to be on many lips
meaning little there
it would be enough for me to know
who is writing this
and sleep knowing it

far from glory and its gibbets

and dream of those who drank at the icy fountain
and told the truth

ENCOUNTER

Name for a curtain at night
sister of some
unfuelled flame

imperious
triumphant and unloved
how did you find the houses
from which now you emanate
in which someone has just

but no sound reaches the gate
here
though all the lights are burning

THE WELL

Under the stone sky the water
waits
with all its songs inside it
the immortal
it sang once
it will sing again
the days
walk across the stone in heaven
unseen as planets at noon
while the water
watches the same night

Echoes come in like swallows
calling to it
it answers without moving
but in echoes
not in its voice
they do not say what it is
only where

It is a city to which many travellers
came with clear minds
having left everything even
heaven
to sit in the dark praying as one silence
for the resurrection

37

LARK

In the hour that has no friends
above it
you become yourself
voice
black
star burning in cold heaven
speaking well of it
as it falls from you
upward

Fire
by day
with no country
where and at what height
can it begin
I the shadow
singing I
the light

THE BLACK PLATEAU

The cows bring in the last light
the dogs praise them
one by one they proceed through the stone arch
on the chine of the hill
and their reflections in the little
cold darkening stream
and the man with the pole
then the night comes down to its roads
full of love for them

I go eating nothing so you will be one and clear
but then how could you drown
in this arid country of stone and dark dew
I shake you in your heavy sleep
then the sun comes
and I see you are one of the stones

Like a little smoke in the vault
light for going
before the dogs wake in the cracked barn
the owl has come in from his shift
the water in the stone basin has forgotten
where I touch the ashes they are cold
everything is in order

Kestrel and lark shimmer over the high stone
like two brothers who avoid each other
on the cliff corner I met the wind
a brother

Almost everything you look on great sun
has fallen into itself here
which it had climbed out of like prayers
shadows of clouds
and the clothes of old women blow over the barrens
one apple tree still blossoms for its own sake

———

The cold of the heights is not the cold of the valleys
the light moves like a wind
the figures are far away walking slowly
in little knots herding pieces of darkness
their faces remote as the plaster above deaths
in the villages

———

The upper window of a ruin
one of the old faces
many places near here
things grow old where nothing was ever a child

———

Oh blessed goat live goat blessed rat
and neither of you lost

———

There is still warmth in the goat sheds years afterwards
in the abandoned fountain a dead branch points
upwards
eaten out from inside as it appears to me
I know a new legend
this is the saint of the place his present form
another blessing in absence
when the last stone has fallen he will rise
from the water
and the butterflies will tell him what he needs to know
that happened while he was asleep

———

The beginnings and ends of days like the butts of arches
reach for roofs that have fallen
the sun up there was never enough
high in its light
the bird moves apart from his cry

THE APPROACHES

The glittering rises in flocks
suddenly in the afternoon
and hangs
voiceless above the broken
houses
the cold in the doorways
and at the silent station
the hammers
out of hearts
laid out in rows in the grass

The water is asleep
as they say
everywhere
cold cold
and at night the sky
is in many
pieces in the dark
the stars set out
and leave their light

When I wake
I say I may never
get there but should get
closer and hear the sound
seeing figures I go toward them waving
they make off
birds
no one to guide me
afraid
to the warm ruins
Canaan
where the fighting is

THE WHEELS OF THE TRAINS

They are there just the same
unnoticed for years
on dark tracks at the foot of their mountain

behind them holes in the hill
endless death of the sky
foreheads long unlit
illegibly inscribed

the cars
have been called into the air
an air that has gone
but these wait unmoved in their rust
row of suns
for another life

ahead of them
the tracks lead out through tall milkweed
untouched

for all my travels

LACKAWANNA

Where you begin
in me
I have never seen
but I believe it now
rising dark
but clear

later when I lived where
you went past
already you were black
moving under gases by
red windows
obedient child
I shrank from you

on girders of your bridges
I ran
told to be afraid
obedient
the arches never touched you the running
shadow never
looked
the iron
and black ice never
stopped ringing under foot

terror
a truth
lived alone in the stained buildings
in the streets a smoke
an eyelid a clock

a black winter all year
like a dust
melting and freezing in silence

you flowed from under
and through the night the dead drifted down you
all the dead
what was found later no one
could recognize

told to be afraid
I wake black to the knees
so it has happened
I have set foot in you
both feet
Jordan
too long I was ashamed
at a distance

William Bartram how many
have appeared in their sleep
climbing like flames into
your eyes
and have stood gazing out over the sire of waters
with night behind them
in the east
The tall bank where you stood
would soon crumble
you would die before they were born
they would wake not remembering
and on the river
that same day
was bearing off its empty flower again
and overhead the sounds of the earth
danced naked
thinking no one could see them

THE TRAIL INTO KANSAS

The early wagons left no sign
no smoke betrays them
line pressed in the grass *we were here*
all night the sun bleeds in us
and the wound slows us in the daytime
will it heal
there

we few
late
we gave our names to each other to keep
wrapped in their old bells
the wrappings work loose
something eats them when we sleep and wakes us
ringing

when day comes
shadows that were once ours and came back to look
stand up for a moment ahead of us
and then vanish
we know we are
watched but there is no danger
nothing that lives waits for us
nothing is eternal

we have been guided from scattered wombs
all the way here choosing choosing
which foot to put down
we are like wells moving
over the prairie
a blindness a hollow a cold source
will any be happy to see us
in the new home

47

WESTERN COUNTRY

Some days after so long even the sun
is foreign
I watch the exiles
their stride
stayed by their antique faith that no one
can die in exile
when all that is true is that death is not exile

Each no doubt knows a western country
half discovered
which he thinks is there because
he thinks he left it
and its names are still written in the sun
in his age and he knows them
but he will never tread their ground

At some distances I can no longer
sleep
my countrymen are more cruel than their stars
and I know what moves the long
files stretching into the mountains
each man with his gun
his feet
one finger's breadth off the ground

THE GARDENS OF ZUÑI

The one-armed explorer
could touch only half of the country
In the virgin half
the house fires give no more heat
than the stars
it has been so these many years
and there is no bleeding

He is long dead with his five fingers
and the sum of their touching
and the memory
of the other hand
his scout

that sent back no message
from where it had reached
with no lines in its palm
while he balanced
balanced
and groped on
for the virgin land

and found where it had been

HOMELAND

The sky goes on living it goes
on living the sky
with all the barbed wire of the west
in its veins
and the sun goes down
driving a stake
through the black heart of Andrew Jackson

FEBRUARY

Dawn that cares for nobody
comes home
to the glass cliffs
an expression
needing no face
the river flies under cold feathers
flies on
leaving its body
the black streets bare their veins
night
lives on in the uniforms
in the silence of the headlines
in the promises of triumph
in the colors of the flags
in a room of the heart
while the ends and the beginnings
are still guarded
by lines of doors
hand in hand
the dead guarding the invisible
each presenting its message
I know nothing
learn of me

HUCKLEBERRY WOMAN

Foreign voice woman
of unnamed origins nothing
to do with what I was taught
at night when it was nobody's
you climbed the mountain in back of the house
the thorn bushes slept
in their words
before day you put on
the bent back like a hill
the hands at the berries

and I wake only to the crying
when the wash tub has
fallen from your head and the alley
under the window is deep
in the spilled blue of far ranges
the rolling of small
starless skies and you turning
among them key
unlocking the presence
of the unlighted river
under the mountains

and I am borne with you on its
black stream
oh loss loss the grieving
feels its way upward
through daggers of stone
to stone
we let it go it
stays we share it
echoed by a wooden
coughing of oars in the dark

52

whether or not they are ours
we go with the sound

LITTLE HORSE

You come from some other forest
do you
little horse
think how long I have known these
deep dead leaves
without meeting you

I belong to no one
I would have wished for you if I had known how
what a long time the place was empty
even in my sleep
and loving it as I did
I could not have told what was missing

what can I show you
I will not ask you if you will stay
or if you will come again
I will not try to hold you
I hope you will come with me to where I stand
often sleeping and waking
by the patient water
that has no father nor mother

THE PORT

The river is slow
and I knew I was late arriving but had no idea
how late
in the splintery fishing port silence
was waving from the nails
dry long since
the windows though rattling
were fixed in time and space
in a way that I am not nor ever was
and the boats were out of sight

all but one
by the wharf
full of water
with my rotted sea-clothes lashed to a piling
at its head
and a white note nailed there in a can
with white words
I was too late to read

when what I came to say is I have learned who we are

when what I came to say was
consider consider
our voices
through the salt

they waken in heads
in the deaths themselves

that was part of it

when what I came to say was
it is true that in
our language deaths are to be heard
at any moment through the talk
pacing their wooden rooms jarring
the dried flowers
but they have forgotten who they are
and our voices in their heads waken
childhoods in other tongues

but the whole town has gone to sea without a word
taking my voice

PRESIDENTS

The president of shame has his own flag
the president of lies quotes the voice
of God
as last counted
the president of loyalty recommends
blindness to the blind
oh oh
applause like the heels of the hanged
he walks on eyes
until they break
then he rides
there is no president of grief
it is a kingdom
ancient absolute with no colors
its ruler is never seen
prayers look for him
also empty flags like skins
silence the messenger runs through the vast lands
with a black mouth
open
silence the climber falls from the cliffs
with a black mouth like
a call
there is only one subject
but he is repeated
tirelessly

THE FREE

So far from the murders
the ruts begin to bleed
but no one hears
our voices
above the sound of the reddening feet
they leave us the empty roads
they leave us
for companions for messengers
for signs
the autumn leaves
before the winter panes
we move among them
doubly invisible
like air touching the blind
and when we have gone they say we are with them forever

THE PRINTS

Above white paths a bugle
will sound from the top of an unseen wall
and beds be empty as far as eye will reach
made up spotless
the shallow prints where each traveller carried
what he had

whiteness came back to the paths after each
footstep and the travellers
never met in the single files
who deepened the same
shadows

while the snow fell

THE REMOVAL

To the endless tribe

I *The Procession*

When we see
the houses again
we will know that we are asleep at last

when we see
tears on the road
and they are ourselves
we are awake
the tree has been cut
on which we were leaves
the day does not know us
the river where we cross does not taste salt

the soles of our feet are black stars
but ours is the theme
of the light

II *The Homeless*

A clock keeps striking
and the echoes move in files
their faces
have been lost
flowers of salt
tongues from lost languages
doorways closed with pieces of night

III   *A Survivor*

The dust never settles
but through it tongue tongue comes walking
shuffling like breath
but the old speech
is still in its country
dead

IV   *The Crossing of the Removed*

At the bottom of the river
black ribbons cross under
and the water tries to soothe them
the mud tries to soothe them
the stones turn over and over trying
to comfort them
but they will not be healed
where the rims cut
and the shadows
sawed carrying
mourners
and some that had used horses
and had the harness
dropped it in half way over
on the far side the ribbons come out
invisible

v   *A Widow Is Taken*

I call leave me here
the smoke on the black path
was my children
I will not walk
from the house I warmed
but they carry me through the light
my blackening face
my red eyes
everywhere I leave
one white footprint
the trackers will follow us into the cold
the water is high
the boats have been stolen away
there are no shoes
and they pretend that I am a bride
on the way to a new house

vi   *The Reflection*

Passing a broken window
they see
into each of them the wedge of blackness
pounded
it is nothing
it splits them
loose hair
bare heels
at last they are gone
filing on in vacant rooms

THE OLD ROOM

I am in the old room across from the synagogue
a dead chief hangs in the wallpaper
he is shrinking into the patch of sunlight
with its waves and nests and in the silence that follows
his death
the parade is forming again
with the street car for its band
it is forming I hear the shuffling the whispers
the choking then the grinding starts off
slowly as ice melting
they will pass by the house

closed ranks attached to the iron trolley
dragged on their backs
the black sleeves the fingers waving like banners
I am forbidden to look
but the faces are wrapped except for the eyes
darkness wells from the bandages
spreads
its loaves and fishes while on the curbs
the police the citizens
of all ages beat the muffled street with bars

what if I call *It is not me* will it stop
what if I raise an arm
to stop it
I raise an arm the whole arm stays white
dry as a beach
little winds play over it
a sunny and a pleasant place I hold it
out it leaves me it goes toward them
the man in charge is a friend of the family

he smiles when he sees it he takes its hand
he gives it its bar
it drops it
I am forbidden to look

I am in the old room across from the stone star
the moon is climbing in gauze
the street is empty
except for the dark liquid running
in the tracks of ice
trying to call
Wait
but the wires are taken up with the election
there is a poll at the corner I am not to go in
but I can look in the drugstore window
where the numbers of the dead change all night on the wall
what if I vote *It is not me* will they revive
I go in my father has voted for me
I say no I will vote in my own name
I vote and the number leaps again on the wall

I am in the old room across from the night
the long scream is about to blossom
that is rooted in flames
if I called *It is not me* would it reach
through the bells

THE NIGHT OF THE SHIRTS

Oh pile of white shirts who is coming
to breathe in your shapes to carry your numbers
to appear
what hearts
are moving toward their garments here
their days
what troubles beating between arms

you look upward through
each other saying nothing has happened
and it has gone away and is sleeping
having told the same story
and we exist from within
eyes of the gods

you lie on your backs
and the wounds are not made
the blood has not heard
the boat has not turned to stone
and the dark wires to the bulb
are full of the voice of the unborn

SHOE REPAIRS

For Charles Hanzlicek

Long after the scheduled deaths of animals
their skins made up into couples
have arrived here
empty
from many turnings
between the ways of men
and men

In a side street
by brown walls over a small light
the infinite routes
which they follow a little way
come together
to wait in rows in twos
soles
eyes of masks
from a culture lost forever

We will know the smell
in another life
stepping down
barefoot into this Ark
seeing it lit up but empty
the destined racks
done with the saved pairs
that went out to die each alone

A G E

These fields of thistles are the old
who believed in the day they had
and held it like an army
now that they are blind
with an alien whiteness clutching their feet
their hair blows into the sea

Ancient sockets
as the snow fell you looked up
full of milk
saying there was something we did not find
it was a child
how could we recognize it since it was never born

As they enter extinction the birds join the vast
flocks of prayers circling over the gulf
in the unreturning light
and the old think it is snow
falling slowly and stopping in the day sky
or the stars the stars

LAUGHTER

The great gods are blind or pretend to be

finding that I am among men I open my eyes
and they shake

SNOWFALL

For my mother

Some time in the dark hours
it seemed I was a spark climbing
the black road
with my death helping me up
a white self helping me up
like a brother
growing
but this morning
I see that the silent kin I loved as a child
have arrived all together in the night
from the old country
they remembered
and everything remembers
I eat from the hands
of what for years have been junipers
the taste has not changed
I am beginning
again
but a bell rings in some village I do not know
and cannot hear
and in the sunlight snow drops from branches
leaving its name in the air
and a single footprint

brother

BANISHMENT IN WINTER

For Richard Howard

From the north the wands the long
questions of light
descend among us from my country
even by day
and their discoveries are recorded
beyond the silence
blue eyes watch needles
oh little by little it will be seen who remembers
the cold dusk crossing the pastures
the black hay ridged
along the darkness
the color of snow
at night
So even by day
the wands reach toward the outer river
toward the deep shadows
inquiring and above us
like stars in a slow negative
the migrants
the true migrants
already immeasurably far
the dark migrants
the souls
move outward into the cold
but will it ever be
dark again in my country
where hanging from lamp posts
the good
fill the streets with their steady light

FOOTPRINTS ON THE GLACIER

Where the wind
year round out of the gap
polishes everything
here this day are footprints like my own
the first ever
frozen
pointing up into the cold

and last night someone
marched and marched on the candle flame
hurrying
a painful road
and I heard the echo a long time afterwards
gone and some connection of mine

I scan the high slopes for a dark speck
that was lately here
I pass my hands
over the melted wax
like a blind man
they are all
moving into their seasons at last
my bones face each other trying
to remember a question

nothing moves while I watch
but here the black trees
are the cemetery of a great battle
and behind me as I turn
I hear names leaving the bark
in growing numbers and flying north

T A L E

After many winters the moss
finds the sawdust crushed bark chips
and says old friend
old friend

FULL MOONLIGHT IN SPRING

Night sends this white eye
to her brother the king of the snow

NIGHT WIND

All through the dark the wind looks
for the grief it belongs to
but there was no place
for that any more

I have looked too
and seen only the nameless hunger
watching us out of the stars
ancestor

and the black fields

MIDNIGHT IN EARLY SPRING

At one moment a few old leaves come in
frightened
and lie down together and stop moving
the nights now go in threes
as in a time of danger
the flies
sleep like sentries on the darkened panes

some alien blessing
is on its way to us
some prayer ignored for centuries
is about to be granted to the prayerless
in this place

who were you
cold voice born in captivity
rising
last martyr of a hope
last word of a language
last son
other half of grief
who were you

so that we may know why
when the streams
wake tomorrow and we are free

AS THOUGH I WAS WAITING
FOR THAT

Some day it will rain
from a cold place
and the sticks and stones will darken their faces
the salt will wash from the worn gods
of the good
and mourners will be waiting
on the far sides of the hills

and I will remember the calling
recognized at the wrong hours
long since
and hands a long way back
that will have forgotten
and a direction will have abandoned my feet
their way
that offered
itself vainly day after day
at last gone
like a color or the cloth at elbows

I will stir when it is getting dark
and stand when it is too late
as though I was waiting for that
and start out into the weather
into emptiness
passing the backs of trees
of the rain of the mourners
the backs of names the back
of darkness

for no reason
hearing no voice
with no promise
praying to myself
be clear

THE PLUMBING

For Adrienne Rich

New silence
between the end and the beginning
The planet that was never named
because it was dark
climbs into the evening
nothing else moves
moon stars the black laundry the hour
have stopped and are looking away
the lungs stand
a frozen forest
into which no air comes

they go on standing like shadows
of the plumbing
that is all that is left
of the great city
the buildings vanished the windows
extinct the smoke with its strings of names
wiped away
and its fire
at the still note
the throwing of a switch

only these pipes
bereft of stairs of elevators
of walls of girders
awakened from lamps from roofs
grow into the night
crowding upward in rows
to desolate heights their blind hope
and their black mouths locked open hollow stars

78

between the dark planets
a famine a worship the heirs
of the dials

among their feet
my heart is still beating by itself
thinking it understands and might feed them

BEGINNING OF THE PLAINS

On city bridges steep as hills I change countries
and this according to the promise
is the way home

where the cold has come from
with its secret baggage

in the white sky the light flickering
like the flight of a wing

nothing to be bought in the last
dim shops
before the plain begins
few shelves kept only by children
and relatives there for the holiday
who know nothing

wind without flags
marching into the city
to the rear

I recognize the first hunger
as the plains start
under my feet

ASCENT

I have climbed a long way
there are my shoes
minute larvae
the dark parents
I know they will wait there looking up
until someone leads them away

by the time they have got to the place
that will do for their age
and are in there with nothing to say
the shades drawn
nothing but wear
between them

I may have reached the first
of the bare meadows
recognized in the air
the eyes by their blankness
turned
knowing myself seen by the lost
silent
barefoot choir

THE HULK

The water itself is leaving the harbor
a gleam waiting in lines
to be gone
and there I am
the small child the small child
alone with the huge ship at last

It must be named for silence
the iron whale asleep on its side
in the breathless port
a name rusted out
in an unknown
unknown language

And no one will come
to call me by any name
the ropes end like water
the walls lie on their backs
bodies dusted with light
I can sail if we sail
I can wander
through the rusting passages forever
with my fear by the hand
by the hand
and no father

FEAR

Fear
there is
fear in fear the name the blue and green walls
falling of and numbers fear the veins that
when they were opened fear flowed from and
these forms it took a ring a ring a ring
a bit of grass green swan's down gliding on
fear into fear and the hatred and something
in everything and it is my death's
disciple leg and fear no he would not
have back those lives again and their fear as
he feared he would say but he feared more he
did not fear more he did fear more
in everything it is there a long time
as I was and it is within those
blue and green walls that the actual
verification has and in fact will
take the form of a ring a ring a ring
took I should say the figure in the hall
of the glass giants the third exhibition
on the right is fear I am I fear and
the rain falling fear red fear yellow fear
blue and green for their depth etcetera
fear etcetera water fire earth air
etcetera in everything made of
human agency or divine fear is
in the answer also and shall pierce thy
bosom too fear three gathered together
four five etcetera the brighest day
the longest day its own fear the light
itself the nine village tailors fear
their thread if not their needles if not
their needles in everything and it is

Fear

here this is New York and aside from that
fear which under another name in
every stone Abraham is buried it
is fear the infant's lovely face the
grass green alleys oh at about the third
hour of the night it being in those parts
still light there came fear my loving fear
in everything it is next the baker the
candlestick maker if you know what I
answer at that point and fear the little
cobbler his last is one fear and there is
fear in all shoes in the shoe line the clothes
line any clothes the blood line any in
everything it is the third button
the book books fear the bottle and what it
contains everything a life death the spirit
staring inward on nothing there and
the sunken vessel the path through the shadow
the shadow of me me or if I am not
suddenly fear coming from the west
singing the great song there was no need
fear no crying and others would sift
the salt in silence in fear the house
where I am familiar in all your
former lives remembered your parents
fear and fear theirs of your parents by
your parents and for your parents shall not
perish from this deciding everything
and it is deciding strike out Mr
Mrs Miss I am alone little stones
fear forgetting forgets remembering
it is my loving fear the mouth of my
seeing fear I am awake I am not
awake and fear no bones like my own
brother fear my death's sister and high on

the cliff face the small arched door from which
a man could fear or be in the winking
of an eye the tapping of the second
finger of the left hand the wind itself
fear I am alone forever I am
fear I am alone I fear I am
not alone couldn't tell your breath from fear
for it is your breath I do it and I'm
supposed to explain it too I fear I
completed my fear in everything there is
fear and I would speak for myself but fear
says logic follows but I advance in
everything and so discovery
geography history law comedy
fear law poetry major prophets
minor prophets that pass in the night
it is a mother and a guiding light
moving across fear before which they burn
in rows in red glass bleeding upwards their
hearts smoke in the gusts on earth as it is
in heaven with the sentence beginning
before the heavens were or the earth
had out of fear been called and any began
to be fear the bird feather by feather
note by note eye by eye pierced he is my
neighbor in the uttermost parts of aye
and shall I couple heaven when the fear
shall fear and those who walked in fear shall see
fear their very form and being for
their eyes shall be opened it was going
on in everything and I forgot but if you
stand here you can see fear the new building
starting to rise from which our children
will fear the stilted dogs the insects
who do not exist the dead burning

Fear

as candles oh dark flames cold lights in
everything without you the ship coming
in and a long way that I would never
traverse before fear had followed that
scent faster than a mortal bearing fear
I'm telling you I'm asking you I'm dying
I'm here today this is New York I'm more
than any one person or two persons
can stand fear the way down in everything
the way up is the same fear the next place
the next I said fear come on you it's you
I'm addressing get into line you're going
never fear there is a hair hanging by
everything it is the edges of things
the light of things do you see nothing
in them burning and the long crying
didn't you hear that either I mean
you again fear it's a strange name not
for a stranger ma'am he said lying I
mean there is you fear me fear but you
must not imagine fear through which the present
moves like a star that I or that
you either clearly and from the beginning
could ever again because from the beginning
there is fear in everything and it is
me and always v s in everything it
is me

PILATE

It has
a life of its own however long it
served Pharaoh and so a heaven of its
own to which its own blood calls which should be
heard with respect when they call crucify
crucify him of its own why should you
not see it unless it is walking arm
in arm with objects which you think you can see
without it when lo empire itself
is not visible

and a future of its own
the prophecies waking without names in
strange lands on unborn tongues those syllables
resurrected staring is that heaven
all the pain to find its hands again old
but you must not suppose that because of
the centurions' reports eclipses
on frontiers and the beards there blowing
through wooden fences dead men but there no
flies in that wind crying sand only
the long arrows and the kissing arrows
through which his wife coming with her spillage
of dreams because of this man but it is
the broken windows that look to the future
and empire is the viewing as different
so a dream itself and how can a man voyage
on more than one bark one trireme one skiff
with one oar at one time even after
the washing is heard on that shore and
the one oar

and you should not imagine either
that you yourselves are later or far or
otherwise else above all those tongues tongues
lit at the tops of arms under
the lungless banners the dread in amber
the silence rolling on before the shadows
burning on the walls with dark cries or going
home a long way through the baths
the gowns dripping the feet growing barer
and the dark flights vanishing into the
cracks in the day

it is termed an alien
judgment they are like that and can force then
be held accountable that has no life
of its own the dark wine dark throats the call
the call that hangs in the banners until
it falls as shall the banners fall
from the walls the walls from the sky its smoke
its eagles what was I put here to change
I was not put here to change

could I change myself my hands
and their dreams a life of their own with its
own heaven own future own windows
washing can I change what they do before
I am born for they will do it without me
arm in arm with objects but lo myself
is not visible to these this man the life
of its own without me its smoke its eagles
and wooden fences and tonight the hands
in the outer circles of the soldiers'
corner fires later than the last meal
gesturing in the reeling night washing
in darkness afterwards will go home

and the darkness will let itself down
into their prayers

SHORE

We turned hearing the same note
of the flute far inland unfaltering and
unknown to each other but already
wrapped in the silence that we would each wear
we left two the hills one the valley before
day entered the pearl and we drew
together as streams descend through their
darkness to the shore

there it was even then by that horn light
of an old skin to be seen approaching
out of the black the lifted prow which waves
touched and fled from on the engraved flood
the scar on the wooden breast climbing above
the breast and the after vessel gazing
up and back at the night the family
the resemblance invisible to us
as it bore in bore in rapidly
to the rocky plain the eggs of venerable
stones the leaden shingle washed and washed under
the shrieks of curlews and that unbreaking
note as of a planet

making in fast toward our eyes fixed
on the uncolored bow one massed and older
jutting in velvet hat and the gown dark
to the shingle beyond whom the sky
whitened out of the gnarled littoral
the other no nearer the waves still young
a fisherman bareheaded in boots
it is my feet that are bare and others
may have gathered behind us the fires

would have been lit at home but we no longer
see behind us

and we hear nothing above the haul
of tongues leaving the shore to the flute's
accompaniment silent flocks pass
on their black journeys it is making in
at a speed that ignores the steely elements
we are waiting waiting what it was carrying
in the early hours as we believed
it could no longer have borne living when the white
shadow gained on heaven and a figure
like the beam of a lantern seemed
to stand in the bark but now though the hollow
board is plainly nearer the light will set
soon where it first rose and we get by heart
the spot where the shingle will scrape in the night
if the keel touches

PSALM: OUR FATHERS

I am the son of joy but does he know me
I am the son of hope but he ascends into heaven
I am the son of peace but I was put out to nurse
I am the son of grief after the brother was lost but I have opened
   an eye in the life where it was he who lived
I am the son of a shadow and I draw my blinds out of respect but
   I cleave uneasily to the light
I am the son of love but where is my home and where the black
   baptismal cup and the frightened eyes that would still come
   to the names I gave them
I am the son of the tribe of Apher which set up empty tents and
   camped where it could defend them and was remembered
   for them but I have discovered that the unknowable needs
   no defense
I am the son of the temptations of the rocks but there have been
   some between
I am the son of fear but I find out for myself
I am the son of the first fish who climbed ashore but the news has
   not yet reached my bowels
I am the son of three flowers the pink the rose and the other or
   its effigy in skin for neither of which was I taught a name
   and I shudder at their withering all three but they will sur-
   vive me
I am the son of the future but she shows me only her mourning
   veil
I am the son of the future but my own father
I am the son of the future but where is my home and the black
   baptismal cup and the warning voice from the bushes under
   the kitchen window saying that they were not my parents
I am the son of a glass tombstone in a fresh plowed field whose
   furrows sit in rows studying the inscriptions of dew the sole
   name life tears as the sun rises but there are no more voices
   on that river

I am the son of the water-thief who got away and founded a
bare-faced dynasty but the fountains are still following
I am the son of a plaster bone in the oldest reconstruction in Mil-
lenial Hall but all my ages are one
I am the son of the cymbal of Bethel that answered like a cracked
bowl to the instruments of ivory of bone iron wood brass
hair gold gut glass through all the generations of the sacred
orchestra a maimed voice before the throne with waiting as
it was for its like to be found its twin its other face sun
socket identical disc the very metal the other half its cymbal
so that it could sound its own true note
but only one had been made
I am the son of an unsuspected wealth but I may labor all my life
and leave nothing but a grain of mustard seed
I am the son of thanksgiving but its language is strange in my
mouth
I am the son of the glove of an upper river and the glove of a tree
but there were four rivers all told around the garden and I
tasted of salt from the beginning
I am the son of the fourth son in the right hand jars on the sec-
ond row of the seventh shelf above the glass footwalk on
the fifth floor in the ninth bay of the eighty third room of
the T18 wing of the heart division of the St. Luke's Memo-
rial Index but he died in a strange land before I was born
I am the son of Cargarran who was an ant in the time of the nose-
less emperors and was accorded great emulation an urn of
amber and a flag to fly his picture on for he fought with the
plague of crane seeds until darkness came to his rescue but
I have use to be frightened if I wake if I remember if a tax is
mentioned or it is Thursday
I am the son of seven promises the last of them to live to see it
again but the womb may not have been listening
I am the son of the word Still after the angels came to the door
in her barren age but on that same day she lost her memory
and she gave birth without understanding

I am the son of a drunken rape at a veterans' convention in a
   brutal empire bandaged with the arguments of empires
   but hallowed be thy name
I am the son of the starvation of the Utes the tortures and gassing
   of the Jews the interrogation of suspects the burning of vil-
   lages the throat of the antelope the amputations of the do-
   mesticated the cries of the extinct and I plead ignorance
   ignorance but it would be no better to be an orphan
I am the son of the ark that was carried empty before the
   tribes in the wilderness but I walk because the times have
   changed and there is no one behind
I am the son of the statue of Hamalid the Great The Weight of
   God that was re-named Vengeance in a different tongue
   and that with raised knife still shouts its incomprehensible
   syllable to the dark square with one foot on the illegible
   date of death and no apparent sex any longer but it was
   modelled on a jailer's dead wife
I am the son of four elements fire darkness salt and vertigo but I
   dance as though they were strangers
I am the son of the cloud Cynian that appeared as a torn white
   breast above Herod and was not recognized but I acknowl-
   edge its vatic suffering still visible in the bruised haze of the
   ridges
I am of the blood of the ash shrew whose remains have not been
   found but whose characteristics have been deduced from
   my teeth my mistakes the atrophied ear at the heart of each
   of my fingerprints and the size of the door at the base of the
   skull where now the performers enter each with his eye
   fixed on the waiting instrument
I am the son of the bird fire that has no eyes but sings to itself
   after waiting alone and silent in the alien wood
I am the son of fear but it means I am never lost
I am the son of terrible labors but triumph comes to the flags that
   have done nothing
I am the son of pain but time nurses me

I am the son of nobody but when I go the islands turn black

I am the son of the first Sabbath but after me cometh the eighth
day

I am the son of hunger hunger and hunger in an unbroken line
back to the mouths of the coelenterates but even I have been
filled

I am the son of remorse in a vein of fossils but I might not have
been

I am the son of division but the nails the wires the hasps the bolts
the locks the traps the wrapping that hold me together are
part of the inheritance

I am the son of indifference but neglect is a stage in the life of the
gods

I am the son of No but memory bathes its knowledge in desire

I am the son of blindness but I watch the light stretch one wing

I am the son of a silence in heaven but I cried and the dark angels
went on falling

I am the son of things as they are but I know them for the most
part only as they are remembered

I am the son of farewells and one of me will not come back but
one of me never forgets

I am the son of violence the ignorant herald but the seal is royal

I am the son of stars never seen never to be seen for we will be
gone before their light reaches us but the decisions they de-
mand are with us
now now

I am the son of love but I lose you in the palm of my hand

I am the son of prisoners but I was got out in the form of a gold
tooth a picture of two elders in a platinum locket a pair of
eyeglasses with rims of white metal one pearl earring a knife
with a picture of Jerusalem on the silver handle and I am be-
ing reassembled and keep finding myself and beginning
again the process of reunion

I am the son of hazard but does my prayer reach you o star of
the uncertain

95

I am the son of blindness but nothing that we have made watches
us

I am the son of untruth but I have seen the children in Paradise
walking in pairs each hand in hand with himself

I am the son of the warder but he was buried with his keys

I am the son of the light but does it call me Samuel or Jonah

I am the son of a wish older than water but I needed till now

I am the son of ghosts clutching the world like roads but tomor-
row I will go a new way

I am the son of ruins already among us but at moments I have
found hope beyond doubt beyond desert beyond reason and
such that I have prayed O wounds come back from death
and be healed

I am the son of hazard but go on with the story you think is
yours

I am the son of love but the hangmen are my brothers

I am the son of love but the islands are black

I am the son of love for which parent the blood gropes in dread
as though it were naked and for which cause the sun hangs
in a cage of light
and we are his pains

CUCKOO MYTH

Stay with the cuckoo I heard
then the cuckoo I heard
then I was born

cuckoo cuckoo she
that from hiding
sings
from dark coverts
from gates where ghosts
stand open
cuckoo
from loss the light rises
a voice that bears with it its hiding

cuckoo that in her time
sings unseen
because the wing beheld
by the unhappy
shall fall
flew again to the first season
to the undivided
returned from there bringing
to the creatures Love
a light for the unhappy
but the light bore with it
its hiding

cuckoo that sings
in echoes
because the voice that the falling follow
falls
flew again under the years
to the unturning

Cuckoo Myth

returned from there bringing
to the world Death
a light for the unhappy
but a light rising
from loss

cuckoo cuckoo
that through time sings changing
now she has gone again

SECOND PSALM: THE SIGNALS

When the ox-horn sounds in the buried hills
    of Iceland
    I am alone
    my shadow runs back into me to hide
    and there is not room for both of us
    and the dread
when the ox-horn sounds on the blue stairs
    where the echoes are my mother's name
    I am alone
    as milk spilled in a street
    white instrument
    white hand
    white music
when the ox-horn is raised like a feather in one
    of several rivers
    not all of which I have come to
    and the note starts toward the sea
    I am alone
    as the optic nerve of the blind
    though in front of me it is written
    This is the end of the past
    Be happy
when the ox-horn sounds from its tassels of blood
    I always seem to be opening
    a book an envelope the top of a well
    none of them mine
    a tray of gloves has been set down
    beside my hands
    I am alone
    as the hour of the stopped clock
when the ox-horn is struck by its brother
    and the low grieving denial
    gropes forth again with its black hands

I am alone
as one stone left to pray in the desert
after god had unmade himself
I am
I still am
when the ox-horn sounds over the dead oxen
the guns grow light in hands
I the fearer
try to destroy me the fearing
I am alone
as a bow that has lost its nerve
my death sinks into me to hide
as water into stones
before a great cold
when the ox-horn is raised in silence
someone's breath is moving over my face
like the flight of a fly
but I am in this world
without you
I am alone as the sadness surrounding
what has long ministered to our convenience
alone as the note of the horn
as the human voice
saddest of instruments
as a white grain of sand falling in a still sea
alone as the figure she unwove each night alone

alone
as I will be

THE PENS

In the city of fire the eyes
look upward
there is no memory
except the smoke writing writing *wait*
wai
w
under the light that has
the stars inside it
the white
invisible stars they also
writing

and unable to read

THE FORBEARS

I think I was cold in the womb
shivering I
remember
cold too I think did my brother suffer
who slept before me there
and cold I am sure was John in the early
as in the earlier
dawn all they
even whose names are anonymous
now known for their cold only
I believe they quaking lay
beforetime there
dancing like teeth and I
was them all foretelling me
if not the name the trembling
if not the time the dancing
if not the hour the longing
in the round night

V O I C E

For Jane Kirstein   1916–1968

By now you will have met
no one
my elder sister
you will have sat
by her breath in the dark
she will have told you I don't know what
in the way she remembers whatever it is
that's how she is
I never see her
but it's you I miss

by now she'll have sat around you
in a circle holding your hand
saying she's listening but
you'll hear you'll hear what she says
to everyone but especially to my friends
is it good what she tells you
is it anything I'd know

her own brother
but I still remember only
afterwards
and we're all like this

by now
more and more I remember
what isn't so
your voice
as I heard it in a dream
the night you died
when it was no longer yours

LAST PEOPLE

Our flowers are numbered
we no longer know where
phrases
last messages written on the white petals
appear as they wither
but in whose language
how could we ask

other messages emerge in the smells
we listen
listen
as they grow fainter

when we go home
with what we have got
when we climb the stairs reciting ancient deeds
the seas grow deeper
that we rose from
when we open the door
when we shut the door
the dust
goes on falling in our heads
goes on falling in our hearts

at the day's end
all our footsteps are added up
to see how near

what will be left
how long will the old men's kingdom survive
the lines of pebbles signifying
house
tea cups on stones

who will feed the dogs
it was like this before

it was like this before
triumphs long in the preparing
stumbled through cracking
film light
and we seem to have known
their faces crumpling just before
they vanished
like papers burning
while the features of plants rose out of plants
to watch them pass
to remember

THIRD PSALM:
THE SEPTEMBER VISION

For Galway Kinnell

I see the hand in which the sun rises
  a memory looking
  for a mind
I see black days black days
  the minds of stones
  going
  but likewise coming
  their sealed way
I see an empty bird cage
  a memory looking
  for a heart
  asked to feel more
  feels less
I see an empty bird flying
  and its song follows me
  with my own name
  with the sound of the ice
  of my own name
  breaking
I see the eyes of that bird
  in each light
  in rain
  in mirrors
  in eyes
  in spoons
I see clear lakes float over us
  touching us with their hems
  and they carry away secrets
  they never brought

I see tongues being divided
    and the birth of speech
    that must grow
    in pain
    and set out for Nineveh
I see a moth approaching
    like one ear of an invisible animal
    and I am not calling
I see bells riding dead horses
    and there was never a silence like this

    oh objects come and talk with us while you can

AFTER THE HARVESTS

Every night hears the sound of rain
it is the roofer's widow looking for him
in her glass sleep

NOW IT IS CLEAR

Now it is clear to me that no leaves are mine
no roots are mine
that wherever I go I will be a spine of smoke in the forest
and the forest will know it
we will both know it

and that the birds vanish because of something
that I remember
flying from me as though I were a great wind
as the stones settle into the ground
the trees into themselves
staring as though I were a great wind
which is what I pray for

it is clear to me that I cannot return
but that some of us will meet once more
even here
like our own statues
and some of us still later without names
and some of us will burn with the speed
of endless departures

and be found and lost no more

MAN WITH ONE LEAF IN OCTOBER NIGHT

The leaves turn black when they have learned how to fly
so does the day
but in the wind of the first hours of darkness
sudden joy sent
from an unknown tree
I have not deserved you

WOMAN FROM THE RIVER

I thought it was an empty doorway
standing there by me
and it was you
I can see that you stood that way
cold as a pillar
while they made the stories about you

LATE NIGHT IN AUTUMN

In the hills ahead a pain is moving its light
through the dark skies of a self
it is on foot I think
it is old
the year will soon be home and its own hear it
but in some house of my soul
a calling is coming in again off the cold mountains
and here one glove is hanging from each window
oh long way to go

STILL AFTERNOON LIGHT

Known love standing in deep grove
new love naked on plain

dance record
from before I was born

played with a new needle

no dancing

KIN

Up the west slope before dark
shadow of my smoke
old man

climbing the old men's mountain

at the end
birds lead something down to me
it is silence

they leave it with me
in the dark
it is from them

that I am descended

MEMORY OF SPRING

The first composer
could hear only what he could write

SIGNS

Half my life ago
watching the river birds

———

Dawn
white bird let go

———

Strange
to be any place

———

Leaves understand flowers
well enough

———

Each sleeper
troubled
by his light

———

Waves sever
sever

———

Silence
is my shepherd

———

Born once
born forever

———

Small dog barking
far down in walls

———

The wind wakes in the dark
knowing it's happened

———

Music stops
on the far side of a bay

———

Don't walk

———

Window
in the house
of a blind man

———

A shout
darkening the roofs

———

Quick smile
like a shoe's

———

No keys to the shadows
the wind shakes them

———

Silent rivers
fall toward us
without explaining

———

City
stands by a river
with torches

———

Not part of the country
part of the horizon

———

Blind
remembering me as a child

———

Bitterness of seeds
a form of knowledge

———

Signs

Men
until they enter that building

———

Look at their shoes
to see how gravely
they are hurt

———

Deaf
listens for his heart

hears name of a great star
never seen

———

Snow
falls in plum orchards
as though it had been there before

———

Bell spills
sky darkens

———

Appear
not as they are
but as what prevents them

———

Walk

———

Clear night
fish
jumping at stars

THE PAW

I return to my limbs with the first
gray light
and here is the gray paw under my hand
the she-wolf Perdita
has come back
to sleep beside me
her spine pressed knuckle to knuckle
down my front
her ears lying against my ribs
on the left side where the heart beats

and she takes its sound for the pulsing
of her paws
we are coursing the black sierra once more
in the starlight
oh Perdita

we are racing over the dark auroras
you and I with no shadow
with no shadow
in the same place

so she came back
again in the black hours
running before the open sack
we have run
these hours together
again
there is blood
on the paw under my fingers
flowing
there is blood then
on the black heights again

in her tracks
our tracks
but vanishing like a shadow

and there is blood
against my ribs again
oh Perdita
she is more beautiful after every wound
as though they were stars
I know
how the haunches are hollowed
stretched out in the dark
at full speed like a constellation
I hear
her breath moving on the fields of frost
my measure
I beat faster
her blood wells through my fingers
my eyes shut to see her
again
my way

before the stars fall
and the mountains go out
and the void wakes
and it is day

but we are gone

THE THREAD

Unrolling the black thread
through the tunnel
you come to the wide wall
of shoes
the soles standing
out in the air you breathe
crowded from side to side
floor to ceiling
and no names
and no door
and the bodies
stacked before them like bottles
generation upon
generation
upon generation
with their threads
asleep in their hands
and the tunnel is full
of their bodies
from there
all the way to the end of the mountain
the beginning of time
the light of day
the bird
and you are unrolling
the Sibyll's song
that is trying to reach her
beyond your dead

THE BLESSING

There is a blessing on the wide road
the egg shell road the baked highway
there is a blessing an old woman
walking fast following him

pace of a child following him

he left today
in a fast car

until or unless
she is with him
the traffic flows through her
as though she were air
or not there

she can speak only to him
she can tell him
what only he can hear

she can save him
once

it might be enough

she is hurrying

he is making good time
his breath comes more easily
he is still troubled at moments
by the feeling
that he has forgotten something
but he thinks he is escaping a terrible
horseman

BEGINNING

Long before spring
king of the black cranes
rises one day
from the black
needle's eye
on the white plain
under the white sky

the crown turns
and the eye
drilled clear through his head
turns
it is north everywhere
come out he says

come out then
the light is not yet
divided
it is a long way
to the first
anything
come even so
we will start
bring your nights with you

THE FIRST DARKNESS

Maybe he does not even have to exist
to exist in departures
then the first darkness falls
even there a shining is flowing from all the stones
though the eyes are not yet made that can see it
saying Blessèd
are ye

THE CHAFF

Those who cannot love the heavens or the earth
beaten from the heavens and the earth
eat each other
those who cannot love each other
beaten from each other
eat themselves
those who cannot love themselves
beaten from themselves
eat a terrible bread
kneaded in the morning shrouded all day
baked in the dark
whose sweet smell brings the chaff flying like empty hands
through the turning sky night after night
calling with voices of young birds
to its wheat

FOURTH PSALM: THE CEREMENTS

She made him a roof with her hands
    from his own voice she wove
    the walls to stop the wind
    with his own dreams she painted the windows
    each with its kingdom
    and the doors were mirrors she fashioned
    of his eyes

    but when she opened it he was gone

    gone the vision
    gone
    the witness

She made him a cage of wishes
    he helped when he could
    helped long
    and indeed with all the heavy parts

    but when she opened it

She made him a net of consents
    where he might turn in his own place
    like an eye in its veins
    a globe in its hours
    she hung it with tears
    with both of theirs

    but when she opened it he was gone

    gone
    the asking

She made him a box of some sweet wood
    she knew he remembered from his childhood
    in corners rose columns she had painted like smoke
    she drew a star inside the lid

    but when she opened it

She made him a bed such as the fates have
    in the palms of the newly born
    but there they do not lay them down
    they have risen

    and when she opened it
    he was gone

    gone the cry the laughter

They made him a fence of names
    each with its story
    like his own teeth
    they laid claim
    to his ears
    but he had others

    when they opened the echoes even the echoes
    he had gone

They made him an ark of the one tree
    and places for him builded in
    two of every kind

    but before the rain came
    he was gone

laws of the hands gone
night of the veins gone
gone the beating in the temples

and every face in the sky

THE WEB

So it's mine
this leg of a thin gray travelling animal
caught in the web again
tearing
in the stocking of blood

the old scars waking opening
in the form of a web

the seamless fabric itself bleeding
where it clings

and all this time dark wings
cries
cries flying over at a great height

o web

over the sand you are woven
over the water you are woven
over the snow you are woven
over the grass you are woven
over the mountains you are woven
over the heads of the lambs you are woven
over the fish you are woven
over the faces you are woven
over the clouds you are woven
over pain itself you are woven

the tears glint on you like dew
the blood is spreading wherever you have held me
the days and the nights

keep their distance
without a sound

but I remember also the ringing spaces
when I have crossed you like a hand on a harp
and even now
in the echoless sky the birds pursue our music

hoping to hear it again

LETTER

By the time you read this

    it is dark on the next page

    the mourners sleep there
    feeling their feet in the tide

    before me in the dusk an animal rose and vanished
    your name

    you have been with me also in the descent
    the winter
    you remember
    how many things come to one name
    hoping to be fed

    it changes but the name for it
    is still the same
    I tell you it is still the same

    hungry birds in the junipers
    all night
    snow

    all night

    by the time you read this

    the address of the last house
    that we will sleep in together on earth
    will have been paid as a price
    dialled on a telephone
    worn as identification

passed on speedometers in unmarked places
multiplied by machines
divided divided
undistracted
standing guard over us all the time
over past future
present
faceless angel

whom each rain washes nearer to himself

but I tell you
by the time you read this
wherever

I tell you

INSCRIPTION FACING WESTERN SEA

Lord of each wave comes in
campaign finished ten thousand miles
years clashes winds dead moons
riderless horses no messages
he lays down flag bowing quickly and retires
his flag
sun waits to take him home
flag fades
sand
stars gather again to watch the war

THE SADNESS

Thinking of you I lean over silent water
this head
appears
the earth turns
the sky has no motion
one by one my eyelashes free themselves
and fall
and meet themselves for the first time
the last time

THE CALLING UNDER THE BREATH

Through the evening
the mountains approach over the desert
sails from a windless kingdom

silence runs through the birds
their shadows freeze

where are you

where are you where are you
I have set sail on a fast mountain
whose shadow is everywhere

SUNSET AFTER RAIN

Old cloud passes mourning her daughter
can't hear what anyone tells her
every minute is one of the doors that never opened

———

Little cold stream wherever I go
you touch the heart
night follows

———

The darkness is cold
because the stars do not believe in each other

ELEGY

Who would I show it to

Ash tree
sacred to her who sails in
from the one sea
all over you leaf skeletons
fine as sparrow bones
stream out motionless
on white heaven
staves of one
unbreathed music
Sing to me

W. S. Merwin

W. S. Merwin was born in New York City in 1927
and grew up in Union City, New Jersey, and in
Scranton, Pennsylvania. From 1949 to 1951 he
worked as a tutor in France, Portugal, and Majorca.
After that, for several years he made the greater
part of his living by translating from French,
Spanish, Latin and Portuguese. Since 1954 several
fellowships have been of great assistance. In addi-
tion to poetry, he has written articles, chiefly for
The Nation, and radio scripts for the BBC. He has
lived in England, France, and the United States.
His books of poetry are *A Mask for Janus* (1952),
The Dancing Bears (1954), *Green with Beasts*
(1956), *The Drunk in the Furnace* (1960), (avail-
able in one volume as *The First Four Books of
Poems*) *The Moving Target* (1963), *The Lice*
(1967), *The Carrier of Ladders* (1970) for which
he received the Pulitzer Prize, *Writings to an
Unfinished Accompaniment* (1973) and *The Com-
pass Flower* (1977). His translations include *The
Poem of the Cid* (1959), *Spanish Ballads* (1960),
The Satires of Persius (1961), *Lazarillo de Tormes*
(1962), *The Song of Roland* (1963), *Selected
Translations 1948–1968* (1968), for which he won
the P.E.N. Translation Prize for 1968, *Transparence
of the World*, a translation of his selection of poems
by Jean Follain (1969) and (with Clarence Brown)
Osip Mandelstam, Selected Poems (1974). In 1974
he was awarded The Fellowship of the Academy
of American Poets.